Just Passing Through

Printed in the
United States of America
First Printing 1990
ISBN 0–9627726–1–5

Library of Congress Catalog Card Number 90–84171
Copyright 1990 by Blue Crab Press
3 Church Circle, Suite 140
Annapolis, Maryland 21401

3 Church Circle, Suite 140
Annapolis, Maryland 21401

Just Passing Through

Poems by Mick Blackistone
Photographs by Marion E. Warren

*"Man did not weave
the web of life,
he is merely a
strand in it.
Whatever he does
to the web, he does
to himself."*
—Chief Seattle

Just Passing Through

daydreaming
    of blue sky
        and
    open water
uncluttered and free
to seek my bounty
      lying beyond
          beneath
the abyss
     patiently waiting
with teasing illusions
knowing
    I can't stay away
         too long

you remind me of a fresh spring morning
bathed in sunlight
                   and the smell of newborn violets

you remind me of a snowy evening
fresh with life dressed in a white blouse
               gleaming in a moonbeam

You remind me of a misty sea
calm under a shroud of enthusiasm
           waiting to break loose and carry me away

you remind me of life
               so often
that my excitement is overwhelming

finally, you remind me of love and peace
               happiness and warmth
because I receive so much from you
                   Miss Edith

who knows
what's real anymore
as we step
            between
delusion and illusion
our hearts
our minds
our souls
on display
as we try
            to close ourselves off
from
        what's real
                anymore

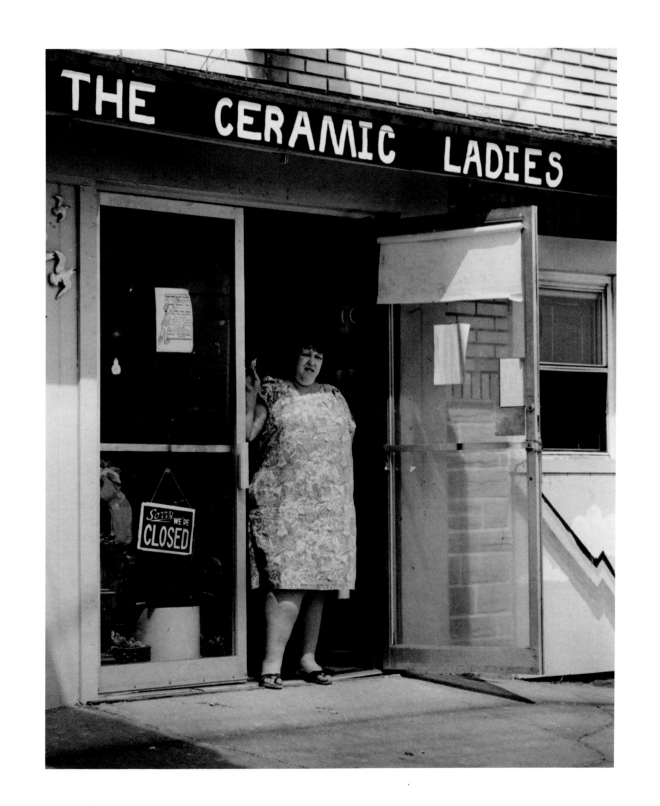

in the throws
of confusion
   frustration
   apprehension
   isolation
   rebellion
my energy burned
         seeking
freedom in flight
there was hope out there
   somewhere anywhere
and then
    quite simply
my search ended
     with you

footsteps tread through the mountain
draped with the mellowing of dawn
silent
     sliding
          footsteps mark the passage
          to where I will meet you
the mountain is beautiful here
sounds are silent
             beneath the power
of the granite rumbling impatiently
in anticipation
          of our meeting
          in its shadow veil
to feel the emotion
            of nature's naked passion

through it all
you were there
 when I needed you
 the most
when
 my vision blurred
and
 my voice cracked
you were there
when
 my strength failed
and
 my heart ached
you were there
surrounded
by familiar strangers
I knew
  I could always
lean on you

"What's the matter with you?" she demanded.
"Make something of yourself!"
"When are you going to straighten up?"

Echoing through
the caverns of my mind
she
    haunts me still
as I
    lie beneath the covers
    in a fetal position
thinking
    about where I'll be
                        tomorrow

Probably hauling oysters
                        from that old river
saying to Miss Katherine's ghost:

"I may straighten up
                one day."

we've walked
many a crooked path
you and me
never could get things straight
                         could we

and
even now
when we thought
they'd never find us
our hide-a-way
at the end of another
          crooked path
we hear the sound
of the bulldozers
                    still

sometimes
            it's good to be home
with friends
and familiar surroundings
back
to what is sacred
where
        the water's voice
is that of your father's
where
        the sand's warmth
is that of your mother's
and the blood
in your veins
                flows through
to your brothers

Sunday
we gather together
as we always have
brothers
            in communion
            offering confession
cleansing our spirits
by
  swapping lies
  telling tales
  bluffing our way through
                    another Sunday

So many men have passed this way
remembering your name
and the memories
                              good and bad
long nights
                    spent with you
                    in quiet company
as you carried their dreams
from here to there
                              and back again
you listened
                    to their fears
                    and tears
                    and laughter
you knew all their secrets
and then
            they would leave
after
      spending time with you
      trusting you
                        would deliver
                        all they expected
and you
            never let them down

time was
    when they ran
    between your shadows
    amidst
        tears and laughter
    which
crowded storefronts
between rows of vegetables
        seed
        tools
        fabrics which wove
them all together
and lifted their spirits
        in paradise
time was
  when they looked
  beyond the edge of town
  to seek
        far reaching heights
and
  left you
        behind

it's hard for me
           to know sometimes
where your thoughts are
because
so often
we are in different places
        at different times
I speculate
        then hesitate
and decide to wait
for you to reach me
because you know
          I'm here
        for you

"Why should I stay?" I asked.
"The answer is here," he said.

"Listen to the silence
broken by
          the muskrat working the grass
          the songs of the cricket
               croak of the frog
               purr of the diesel.
Reach out and embrace the breeze
               the dawn's dampness
               the weathered wood.
Lift your head and smell the marsh
               the saltwater
               remnants of fish and crab.
Open your eyes and see the wonders
               never always changing."

"The answer is here," I said.
"Why would you want to leave?" he asked.

I don't know
about the names of things
or
what makes
        this old world turn

I don't know
about the what and why
or
when people
        chose to walk alone

I don't know
about life or death
or
where you
        might fit in

All I know
is my own heart
when
    I think from time to time
and that I may be here
tomorrow
if you're just passing by
whether
        king or vagabond

like statues
        they were there
from first to last
                    light
and through each new moon
        they were there
silently
        watching
                    waiting
as the world ran by

how long can
that old porch
                    stand the strain

after all
      is said and done
and the great
      philosophers
dissect the intricacies
of the season   our season
               our ins and outs
               our ups and downs
               our depth of commitment
               our resistance to change
we can look them
               straight in the eye
and say
      quite eloquently
hell we know enough
               to get by

quietly nestled
among friends
                I contemplate
your existence
covered
in a cloak of white
facing another dawn
you remain idle

where is the winter rapture
the banging
      loading
      talking
      laughing?
Where are the men
who make footprints
                        on your soul
covered in a cloak of rubber and wool

probably
        nestled quietly
among friends
                contemplating
their existence

rest
    weary in your solitude
knowing
that deep within the marrow
of your soul
lay
the memories of transients
generations
             passed by
you carried their secrets
and
    honor them still
deep within the marrow
                      of your soul

what lies beyond
the bend
          in the road
I don't know

what waits for you
round there
I don't know

what stands here
is all
     I know
but I can walk
               this far
                    with you

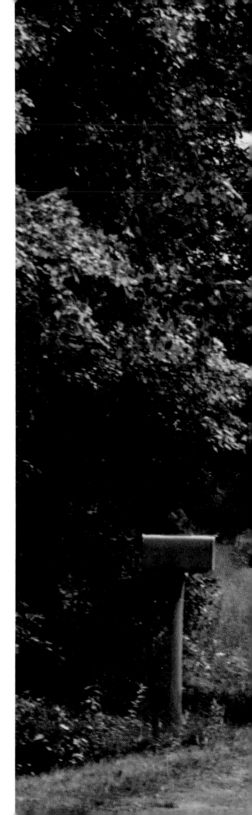

evening
       we are alone now
yellow piercing brown
silky shadows slowly shimmering
                        alone
listening
       watching
           waiting
mother nature
              surrounds us
with her shadow soldiers
I'm glad you are with me
                  alone
listening
       watching
           waiting
for what
the shadows
           come closer now
the cove responds
              to embrace
welcome us
and it's good
           to be among friends
                alone

we spend time
searching
       throughout tomorrow
to find secluded answers
deep within the shadows
           of our minds

we are content in our search
for it is done together
        as one
as it should be
      as we will be
          as we are
and it is good to be together

no. . .

we are not lost
for we are together
in a search to find a way
        there is a way
we know there is a way
together
   so that what we are searching for
we can eventually say
       we found yesterday
          together. . .

if we pause
   will you share
   your wisdom
with us
   as you rest
   your weary mind

if we stop
   will you share
   your thoughts
with us
   so we know
   about the unknown

if we sit
   will you share
   your wealth
with us
   less fortunate
   with little to give
besides
   there's an empty chair
   and we need to be near
                   you

I awoke last night
                around midnight
to eavesdrop on your conversation
you were caught up
                in your own circumstances
and gave
            little consideration
            to my presence
perhaps
            at midnight
I was of little consequence
in the scheme of things
            tonight
            you will be gone
and I
        will be left
                    alone
to recall the conversation
and hope
            for a chance
            to eavesdrop
                        again

they played
            the game for years
then one day
              everything was right
to make a move
and
   we watched   waited
   in anticipation
   anxious
in our own
              anxiety as
this old slowpoke
swallowed his pride
prepared to make a move
on a
    foxy lady
and
we never knew
who came out ahead
neither do they
                but
they're still playing the game
                            today

I've been thinking lately.
Maybe we should make some changes.
Nothing dramatic
                    you understand.
But,
    I suppose,
                    we could do a few things
to make our relationship
a little,
        just a little,
                    more exciting.
I treasure my time with you.
The open relationship,
                times of silent reflection,
                            planning.
Even when I'm furious with you
I'd still rather be with you
                    than somewhere else.
Yea, we should make some changes.
I think they'd make us feel better
even though
                    we feel good now.
Just something small
                    to start with.
So,
  anyway,
        I'll get the paint.

who said
        we couldn't do it
        you and I
as we stood
            in the emptiness
waiting for something
            to lift
            our spirits
and
who said
        we wouldn't make a difference
        you and I
as we took the dare
                through the fear
            between apprehension and
                        self doubt
stepping forward
            to try

hope
moved desperately
taking
      the hand of **faith**
which lingered slowly
stood stoically
with **patience**
          and together
all three helped
push you
closer to your dream

barefoot they ran
      the dreamers and believers
      the schemers and deceivers
the mothers
           of the mothers'
                    children
escaping to you
running from you
trying
      to find their way
and you
      remain
forgotten
but
  for them still

hey
what are you going to do
                              about it?
remain
          asleep   apathetic
or
   run some more?
I didn't ask
               to deserve this
I don't want
               your sympathy
                    compassion
                    understanding
just an answer
               to my question
what are you going to do
                              about it
                                   anyway?
I need to know
               so I can face
                              tomorrow
Please

the sun slips by
and memories
buried beneath furrowed brow
separate
      wheat from chaf
letting me explore
peacefully
the simple
      elegant
          treasures
of my day

This spot
          the here and now
gives us hope
that there can be something
eternal
          left unchanged
by selfish desires
and that
          over time
it will remain
for us
when we return

I suppose
there could be a prettier spot
                              somewhere. . .
but
I can't place it
          right now

what's it to you
         where I go
who hurts me
         secrets I know
the depths of perception
the heights of frustration
I may not
         go anywhere
I may remain
         to myself right here
and hope
         you'll care for me
                  one day

they said
          you were gone
to
more exotic places
bullshit
         I said
have some faith
and then
when
I turned around
you were there
when
     I needed you
                the most

your face
            marks the passage of time
as you follow your mind's eye
to search
            through ancient visions
and
your face
            traces many passages
            with hope
            and
            optimism that there will be
a time and passage
            for your tomorrow

The sun
　　　beat down for centuries
burning through the morning.
They thought
　　　　　you could ignore it
　　　　　and the pain
as you
　　　pulled prodded picked
through
　　　your options
trying to cope
with what your heart
　　　　　　　desired.

How long
　　　have you been out here
　　　　　　　　anyway
　　　out of the way?

```
friends go to the country
          to rest
          and escape
to get away
               from it all
leave problems behind
go
   where time doesn't change much
and values remain the same
               from generation to generation
most stay only
          a short time
it's refreshing
          they say
some stay longer
          become part of the cycle
          from generation to generation
          and
          they are better for it
                              I suppose
```

they say
I might not be able
to work this out
that the times
                are tough
that I'm too old
that the market's
                soft
and the weather's bad
I told them
I've been here
long before
                they thought
of arriving
and
the farm
  was here
long before me
I told them
not to worry about
my hard times
and that
        I'd be happy
to stay on as caretaker
of the land
because
        it's brought me
this far
        and
without their help
thank you

we could do something
            about it
            I suppose
that is
      if we knew
      what it is
      we would do
      something about
and then again
      once we figured it out
we might just decide
      to sit here
      some more
and discuss
            our options

So. . .
          . . .What do you think?
I don't.
So. . .
          . . .What do you feel?
I don't.
So. . .
          . . .What do you know?
I don't.
So. . .
          . . .What do you say?
I don't.
So. . .
          . . .What can I do for you?
Leave me to wait
                    for my friend.

know what?
            no one will know
what went on here
since we've come
                        to this place. . .
left our mark
                lit a spark
did our best
                like the rest
who came
            to this place
                            before us. . .
it's okay
            we know
what went on here and
in the morning
                    we'll be gone. . .

a long time ago
we decided to stay
you and me
stick it out
fighting
      solitude
      drought
      insects
      foreclosure
we could barely stand
      the excitement
and here we are
you and me

it's still exciting
to be with you

I don't know
            things are just different here
it's quiet
      time waits for you
you may catch up
           you may not
I know what it's like
          over there
I lived there
remember
anyway
     for now
I will live here
while
you survive there
        and it's been nice
        talking to you over there

sometimes
when I contemplate
my existence
            where I am
            could have been
my mind
        reaches for your touch
and
   your body
            in my hands
responds
       slowly
            embracing my fingers
and
   I know
       I am happiest
               with you

we have to say good-bye
today
        to generations
of joy and tears
of forgotten dreams
of fading memories
of future plans
it's been a long time
coming
            but we're here now
to watch the crowd
wave good-bye

look
we can't keep fooling around like this
me chasing you
            you avoiding me
we've been carrying on
for too long
and it's time
we got down to terms
with
    destiny
perhaps it was fate
    that brought us together
I don't know
but
now it's time
            to move toward
                        the kitchen

Worry not of yesterday:

It has been lost in the shadows.

Worry not of tomorrow:

It will be found in the sun.

Worry not of today:

It is our celebration for being together.

there's a place
       to search
          seek
          solitude
to find
       or lose
whichever
       choose
up there
       or down here
anywhere
to escape
       or return
to what your heart
               remembers

how long
have you been sitting here
waiting
        reaching
for your life's quota
silently
        swiftly
nimble gnarled fingers
constantly moving
and
the songs
        of generations
break the boredom
set the rhythm
remove you from here
to there
        and back
                tomorrow

Oh Chesapeake
    you mythical mistress
    protecting your children
who come calling
      and crying
helpless without your embrace
accept me
      as a stranger
in your midst
I promise
      I won't be here long

Going through the motions
                    secrets
                    caressing each moment
                    questioning each feeling
tasting the sweat
feeling the pain
                    as muscles tighten
                    withdraw
anticipating completion
                              of your creation
you can give birth
                    with a smile
knowing the ritual
                    will be repeated
                              again

Other Books By Mick Blackistone

The Day They Left The Bay: An exciting children's story about environmental education, with illustrations by Lee Boynton. Winner of the U.S. Environmental Protection Agency Environmental Education Achievement Award, 1989. Ages 6 and up.   Retail $14.95

The Buffalo and the River: A dramatic children's story teaching environmental education through the words of an old Indian, a young boy and a dream vision. Illustrations by Jennifer Heyd Wharton. Ages 8 and up. Retail $14.95

Sun Up To Sundown: Watermen of the Chesapeake: An informative documentary with photographs by James Parker, of the changing lives for men who work the water. In their own words the commercial watermen discuss their way of life and what is affecting them in the 90's.   Retail $19.95

✂--

To order first edition signed copies: Send check or money order to:
 Blue Crab Press, 3 Church Circle, Suite 140, Annapolis, MD 21401
 or call
 301-263-8490
 Maryland residents include 5% sales tax.

The Day They Left The Bay: _____ signed copies at $14.95 each _____ plus tax.

The Buffalo And The River: _____ signed copies at $14.95 each _____ plus tax.

Just Passing Through: _____ signed copies at $13.95 each _____ plus tax.

Sun Up to Sundown: Watermen
 Of The Chesapeake: _____ signed copies at $19.95 each _____ plus tax.

_____ tax (Md. residents)

$3.00 shipping

_____ Total enclosed

For book signings and discount price-list for quantity orders to stores, schools, museums, etc., call 301-263-8490 for further information.